GREAT RIVERS *of*
BRITAIN

THE CLYDE • MERSEY • SEVERN
TEES • THAMES • TRENT

Michael Pollard

Evans Brothers Limited

First published in 1998 by Evans Brothers Limited

Evans Brothers Ltd
2a Portman Mansions
Chiltern Street
London W1U 6NR

Commissioned by: Su Swallow
Consultant: Stephen Watts
Series design: Neil Sayer
Book design: Roger Kohn Designs
Editor: Debbie Fox
Picture research: Victoria Brooker
Maps and diagrams: Hardlines

VISIT OUR WEBSITE
Evans
www.evansbooks.co.uk

British Library Cataloguing in Publication Data.

Pollard, Michael, 1931-
    Great Rivers of Britain
    1.Rivers - Great Britain - Juvenile literature 2.Great
        Britain - History - Juvenile literature
    I.Title
    914.1

ISBN 0 237524813

Printed in China by Midas Printing International Ltd.

The author and publisher wish to thank the following for their help:
Mersey Basin Campaign
Northumbrian Water
North West Water
Scottish Environment Protection Agency
Severn Trent Water
Thames Water
The Environment Agency

ACKNOWLEDGEMENTS

For permission to reproduce copyright material, the author and publishers gratefully acknowledge the following:

Cover (main image) Skyscan Balloon Photography (bottom left) Keith Ringland, Oxford Scientific Films (bottom right) National Watersports Centre, Nottingham **Title page** Collections/Simon Hazelgrove **page 8** (left) P. Davenport/The Edinburgh Photographic Library (right) David Noble **page 9** P. Davenport/The Edinburgh Photographic Library **page 10** (bottom left) Ecoscene/Hodgkinson (right) © IPC Magazines/Robert Harding Picture Library **page 11** (top) Roger Kohn (bottom) Collections/Alan Sparrow **page 12** Keith Ringland, Oxford Scientific Films **page 13** Glasgow Development Agency **page 14** NRSC LTD/Science Photo Library **page 15** Ron Jones Associates/Trafford Park Development Corporation **page 16** Getty Images **page 17** (top) Bluecoat Press (bottom) Collections/Andy Hibbert **page 18** (top left) Trevor Perry/Environmental Images (bottom right) Photo courtesy of United Utilities Picture Library **page 19** (top) Mersey Basin Campaign (bottom) Neville Kuypers/Seacombe Aquarium, Liverpool **page 20** Skyscan Balloon Photography **page 21** Mike Sharp/News Team Birmingham **page 22** (left) Ironbridge Gorge Museum (right) Skyscan Balloon Photography **page 23** Trevor George **page 24** Skyscan Photolibrary **page 25** (top) Paul Glendell/ Environmental Images (bottom) Ecoscene/Sally Morgan **page 26** Collections/Ed Gabriel **page 27** (top) Collections/Philip Nixon (bottom) Collections/Alan Sparrow **page 28** National Railway Museum/Science and Society Picture Library **page 29** Leslie Garland/Environmental Images **page 30** Collections/Mike Kipling **page 31** (top) Tees Barrage and Teesside Whitewater Course, Flagship Schemes of Teesside Development Corporation (middle) North of England Newspapers (bottom) Collections/Mike Kipling **page 32** (top) Skyscan Balloon Photography (bottom) Collectons/Patrick Wise **page 33** (top) CNES, 1995 Distribution Spot Image/Science Photo Library (bottom) Geoffrey Taunton/Sylvia Cordaiy Photo Library **page 34** Getty Images **page 35** (top) David Noble (bottom) Guildhall Library, London/Bridgeman Art Library **page 36** Alex Olah/Environmental Images **page 37** (top left) Skyscan Balloon Photography (top right) Collections/Simon Hazelgrove (bottom) Rex Features **page 38** Collections/Roy Stedall-Humphryes **page 39** Travel Ink/David Toase **page 40** Travel Ink/Ian Booth **page 41 and 42** Photographs provided by Nottingham City Council **page 43** (top) Photographs provided by Nottingham City Council (bottom) Travel Ink/Steve Hines

CONTENTS

JOURNEY OF THE CLYDE

THE CLYDE STARTS ITS JOURNEY TO THE SEA IN THE SOUTHERN UPLANDS OF SCOTLAND AND FLOWS NORTH-WEST TO THE FIRTH OF CLYDE ON THE WEST COAST. ITS LENGTH, FROM ITS SOURCE TO DUMBARTON IN THE CLYDE ESTUARY, IS 170 KILOMETRES.

◀ *The forest-covered Lowther Hills in the Southern Uplands, where the Clyde begins its journey. In winter and spring, the stream running towards the centre of the picture from the bottom right will fill with water and make its way to join the Clyde.*

▶ *Corra Linn, one of the four Falls of Clyde near the village of New Lanark. In 1785, water power from the Falls was used to drive four cotton mills in the village, employing 1600 people.*

THE CLYDE is Scotland's most important river, providing water for over half the country's population. The river collects this water from an area of land called a drainage basin. This basin has a boundary of high land, known as a 'watershed', and all the streams inside the watershed flow through the drainage basin into the main river. These streams are the river's tributaries.

Two streams, Daer Water and Potrail Water, begin on the edge of the watershed in the Lowther Hills, 600 metres above sea level. After travelling northwards through the drainage basin they meet near the village of Elvanfoot to form the Clyde. Daer Water, the longer stream of the two, flows through the Daer Reservoir, where some of the water is stored to supply the towns of Lanarkshire.

FOREST AND FARMLAND

For about 30 kilometres north of Elvanfoot, the upper Clyde flows between thickly forested hills. This is conifer forest, which is regularly harvested and re-planted mainly as raw material for the paper and board industry. Near Lanark, the river reaches the Falls of Clyde, a series of four waterfalls (see page 26) over which the Clyde drops 75 metres in a distance of six kilometres. Since 1927, most of the water has been diverted through a hydro-electric power station, making the Falls of Clyde a less spectacular sight than before.

Below Lanark the narrow valley broadens

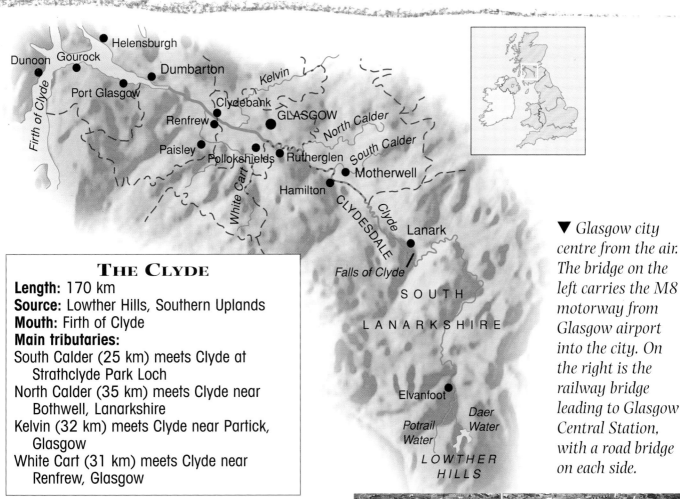

THE CLYDE

Length: 170 km
Source: Lowther Hills, Southern Uplands
Mouth: Firth of Clyde
Main tributaries:
South Calder (25 km) meets Clyde at
    Strathclyde Park Loch
North Calder (35 km) meets Clyde near
    Bothwell, Lanarkshire
Kelvin (32 km) meets Clyde near Partick,
    Glasgow
White Cart (31 km) meets Clyde near
    Renfrew, Glasgow

▼ *Glasgow city centre from the air. The bridge on the left carries the M8 motorway from Glasgow airport into the city. On the right is the railway bridge leading to Glasgow Central Station, with a road bridge on each side.*

out into Clydesdale. This is an area of farmland made fertile by sediment brought down from the hills by the Clyde and its tributary streams. As well as dairy and arable farms, there are orchards and market-gardens growing fruit and vegetables, and plant nurseries and garden centres visited by keen gardeners from the Clyde towns. Lower Clydesdale carries the main road, the M74, linking Glasgow and England as well as the main railway line between Glasgow and London.

SCOTLAND'S LARGEST CITY

As the Clyde approaches Glasgow, its banks are increasingly built-up and it passes large towns such as Motherwell and Hamilton. These grew quickly in the nineteenth century because of the coal and iron ore found nearby.

As the Clyde flows on through Glasgow, hills close in again on each side of the valley. Over the past 200 years Glasgow has spread out from the river banks to cover these hills and become Scotland's largest city with a population of 680,000. West of Glasgow, the Clyde gradually widens to form an estuary lined with docks and harbours. Beyond these are holiday resorts such as Helensburgh and Gourock. Finally, the Firth of Clyde runs southwards to link the river to the Irish Sea and the Atlantic Ocean.

RIVER OF INDUSTRY

UNTIL ABOUT 200 YEARS AGO, THE ONLY MAJOR INDUSTRY ALONG THE CLYDE WAS THE MINING OF LEAD AND SILVER BESIDE THE UPPER REACHES OF ELVAN WATER, WHICH JOINS THE CLYDE AT ELVANFOOT. IN 1801, A DISCOVERY MADE BY A SCOTSMAN CALLED DAVID MUSHET CHANGED ALL THAT.

DAVID MUSHET found that rock in the hills beside the lower Clyde contained both iron and coal. This 'blackband ironstone', as he called it, became the raw material for the making of iron and steel, which was to be the major industry of the Glasgow region for nearly two centuries.

CITY OF ENGINEERING

By 1860, one-third of all British iron was made on the Clyde. The spread of railways throughout Europe meant that there was a huge demand for rails, locomotives, cranes and machinery of all kinds. Factories sprang up to make these and other engineering products from home sewing-machines to ships' engines. The international shipping trade grew quickly too, and shipbuilding became the Clyde's greatest industry. There were 32 kilometres of shipyards along the river where all kinds of craft from tugs and ferry-boats to battleships and ocean liners were built.

THE TEXTILE INDUSTRY

The second great industry that grew up along the Clyde was the spinning, weaving, bleaching, dyeing and printing of cotton. All the manufacturing processes used water from the streams that flowed into the lower Clyde and water powered the industry. The town of Paisley, six kilometres from Glasgow on the west bank of the Clyde, became famous for its printed

▶ *Paisley patterns are based on curved or cone shapes found in plant life. They were first designed by weavers in north-western India.*

◀ *Ravenscraig, Scotland's largest steelworks, which closed in 1992. The closure has improved air and water quality in the area, but the problem of cleaning up contaminated land remains.*

cotton material with highly-coloured and complicated patterns. These had been designed in Norwich in eastern England, but Norwich did not have the factories or the supply of cotton to make large quantities. The chemicals used in bleaching, dyeing and printing were also produced on the Clyde, creating another busy and profitable industry. Today, the Clyde textile industry has almost disappeared because of competition from other textile centres.

THE PORT OF GLASGOW

Imports of raw materials for the industries of the Clyde, and exports of their finished products, turned Glasgow into one of Britain's major ports. The river, which 200 years ago could be crossed by horse and cart in the centre of Glasgow, was deepened in the nineteenth century to take larger ships, and new docks were built in the estuary at Clydebank, Port Glasgow and Renfrew.

As well as this cargo traffic, the Clyde became busy with steamers carrying day-trippers from Glasgow to the holiday towns such as Helensburgh, Gourock and Dunoon along the estuary and along the Firth of Clyde. For thousands of industrial workers, a day 'down the water' was their only holiday.

QUEENS OF THE CLYDE

Of all the ships built on the Clyde, the most famous were the three 'Queen' liners built for the Cunard company. They were designed for the North Atlantic crossing in the days when most travellers between Europe and North America went by sea.

The building of the *Queen Mary* began in 1930. There were 3800 workers in the shipyard and many more were employed by companies supplying materials and fittings. *Queen Mary* was launched in 1934 and made her first voyage in 1937. She is now a floating hotel, conference centre and museum in Long Beach, California. *Queen Elizabeth* (above), begun in 1936, first went to sea in 1940. The ship was destroyed by fire in Hong Kong in 1972. In 1967 *Queen Elizabeth II* was launched. She is still sailing, but is now a cruise ship.

◀ *A Caledonian MacBrayne ferry on its way across the Firth of Clyde from Gourock to Dunoon. A network of ferry routes provides essential transport for remote communities as well as serving tourists.*

CHANGE ON THE CLYDE

THE PAST 30 YEARS HAVE BROUGHT HUGE CHANGES TO THE CLYDE. HEAVY INDUSTRY HAS ALMOST DISAPPEARED, AND THE LAST SHIPBUILDERS ARE THREATENED WITH CLOSURE. BUT NOT ALL THE NEWS IS BAD.

UNTIL 1800, THE CLYDE was a clean river. Within 50 years, industry had turned it into one of the most polluted rivers in Europe. Despite attempts to control the untreated waste that poured into the river from homes and factories, the condition of the Clyde steadily worsened. As late as 1968, the lower Clyde was so polluted that no fish could live in it. Even the upper reaches of the river, which had always been rich in fish such as sea-trout and salmon that swam there from the sea, were affected. These migratory fish could not survive the journey through the polluted lower waters.

▲ *Salmon are saltwater fish that travel from the oceans and swim upstream along rivers to lay their eggs in fresh water. They are sensitive to polluting chemicals and avoid polluted water. This female salmon is making its way upstream to breed and lay its eggs.*

CLEANING UP

A programme to clean up the Clyde began in 1965. It involved building or re-building treatment plants so that waste water was treated before it was allowed to flow into the river. By 1983 there was a sure sign of success. In that year, salmon returned to the Clyde for the first time since about 1860. They have come back every year since. When the huge Ravenscraig steelworks near Motherwell closed in 1992 there was another improvement. It meant that the waste water from the steel-making industry, which contained a high level of poisonous ammonia, was no longer carried downstream.

THE BURRELL COLLECTION
Sir William Burrell was a millionaire Glasgow ship-owner who died in 1958. In 1944 he gave his collection of over 8000 works of art from all over the world to the city of Glasgow, with money to pay for a gallery. At last, in 1983, the Burrell Collection was opened to the public in its new home in Pollokshields on the south side of Glasgow. Today, it attracts thousands of visitors every year.

▲ *Bringing life back to central Glasgow. Old warehouses at Lancefield Quay, on the north bank of the Clyde, were converted to luxury apartments in a £6 million scheme started in 1988.*

However, there are still problems. There are old lead mines along the tributaries of the upper Clyde that still leak lead into the streams, turning the fins and tails of trout black. Although waste water no longer flows from the factories, the land where they stood is still polluted with chemicals that seep into the river. One example is the seepage of chromium from an industrial estate at Rutherglen, just outside Glasgow city centre. The estate is built on land that contains material from an old chromium works. Removing poisonous material from old industrial land is one of the main tasks of environmental agencies today.

THE NEW GLASGOW

'Glasgow – Miles Better' says a large banner that greets drivers approaching the city by road. It is part of a plan to attract new industries to the area and to persuade people that Glasgow is a good place to live.

Port activities and shipbuilding have moved out of central Glasgow to sites downstream where today's larger ships can be berthed. The old sites have been redeveloped to provide riverside walks, parks and gardens. Old warehouses have been converted or replaced as offices and homes. The Scottish Exhibition and Conference Centre has been built on reclaimed dockland.

Other new developments in Glasgow include the Royal Glasgow Concert Hall, opened in 1990, and Tramway, which was converted from a former tram depot as a venue for drama, music and dance.

◀ *'The Armadillo' is the nickname Glasgow people have given to the Clyde Auditorium, a 3000-seater conference centre opened in 1997 on the north bank of the Clyde.*

13

RIVER OF THE NORTH-WEST

THE MERSEY IS THE MAIN RIVER OF NORTH-WEST ENGLAND. IT FLOWS FROM STOCKPORT, NINE KILOMETRES SOUTH-EAST OF MANCHESTER, TO ITS MOUTH ON LIVERPOOL BAY.

THE MERSEY

Length: 112 km
Source: Stockport
Mouth: Liverpool Bay
Main tributaries:
Tame (29 km) and Goyt (24 km) meet at Stockport to form the Mersey
Irwell (48 km) meets Mersey at Irlam, Manchester
Weaver (72 km) meets Mersey near Runcorn
Bollin (32 km) met Mersey near Warburton, now flows into Manchester Ship Canal
Gowy (23 km) flows into Mersey estuary at Stanlow

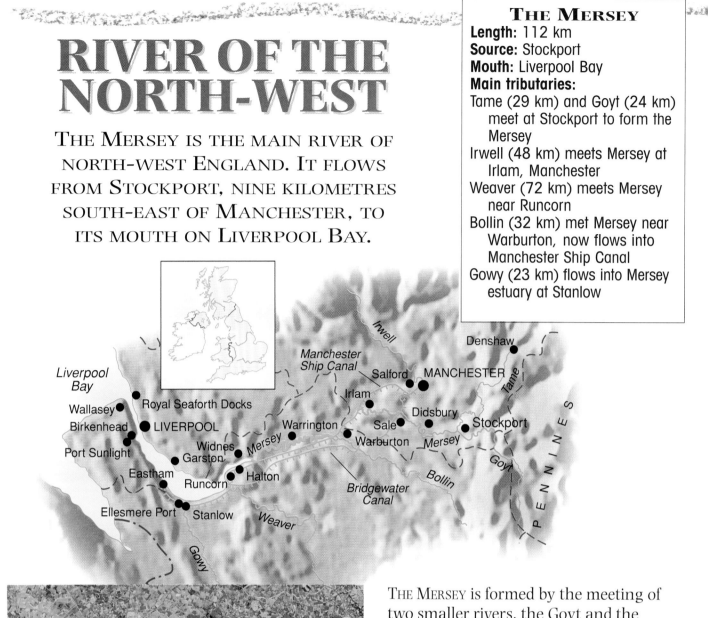

THE MERSEY is formed by the meeting of two smaller rivers, the Goyt and the Tame. These rise in high moorland on the west side of the Pennines, the range of high land that runs from north to south across northern England. The Tame flows south from a reservoir at Denshaw that collects water from the surrounding hills. The Goyt meets it in a narrow, steep-sided gorge at Stockport.

◀ *A satellite image of the lower Mersey, falsely coloured to emphasise particular features. It shows the Mersey from Runcorn and Widnes on the right to Liverpool Bay on the left. The blue area north of the estuary, on the left, is Liverpool, with the Royal Seaforth Docks clearly visible. On the opposite bank is Birkenhead.*

Flood plain and marshland

Humans have changed the course of the Mersey and it is hard now to imagine what the countryside looked like before the towns and cities were built. The Mersey emerged from the gorge at Stockport and flowed across flat land before reaching marshes and the estuary. The flat land is known as a flood plain. During periods of heavy rainfall the Mersey picked up sediment as it flowed out of the Pennines and transported its load - everything the river carries - downstream. When the water level in the river became higher than its banks it overflowed on to the surrounding land - the flood plain. As the water spread out across the plain it lost its power and speed and so deposited most of the sediment it had been carrying, creating the fertile land.

Today, most of the Mersey's course west of Manchester is built up, especially along the main roads, although a few areas of farmland and marsh remain. The twin towns of Runcorn and Widnes, linked by the most westerly bridge across the Mersey, mark the start of the estuary, which, at its widest, is over one kilometre across. On the north bank of the estuary, stretching as far as Liverpool Bay, is Liverpool. On the south side is a string of smaller towns, Ellesmere Port, Birkenhead and Wallasey.

Flood control

Flooding was a frequent problem in the early history of Manchester, and the banks of the Mersey and its tributary the Irwell were built up to control and channel floodwater. Today, overflows of floodwater are trapped in flood basins at Sale and Didsbury, where they are stored and released slowly.

Canals

Canal-building has also altered the character of the Mersey. The first canal to be built in the Mersey valley was from Worsley, about twelve kilometres west of Manchester, into the city. It was opened in 1761. Fifteen years later, the Bridgewater Canal was built, spanning the 40 kilometres between Manchester and Runcorn on the Mersey estuary. These were canals for barges, which could carry only about 50 tonnes of cargo each.

In 1882 a deeper, wider canal was planned to carry the largest ocean-going ships of that time into the heart of Manchester. Fifty-seven kilometres long, the Manchester Ship Canal was opened in 1894, from docks in Manchester and Salford to Eastham on the south side of the Mersey estuary. Now that cargo ships have greatly increased in size, the Manchester end of the canal is less busy. But docks with facilities for handling bulk and container cargoes line the western end from Runcorn through Stanlow and Ellesmere Port to Eastham.

◀ *The Manchester Ship Canal is a minimum of 8.5 metres deep and 36.5 metres wide – wide enough to allow large ships to pass each other easily. It took seven years to build.*

THE MERSEY'S GREAT PORT

FOR 300 YEARS, THE MERSEY AREA HAS BEEN DOMINATED BY ITS GREAT PORT, LIVERPOOL. THE IMPORTS AND EXPORTS ON WHICH MANCHESTER AND THE TOWNS OF LANCASHIRE DEPENDED CAME AND WENT BY SEA DOWN THE MERSEY ESTUARY.

THE CRUEL TRADE OF SLAVERY was Liverpool's first success in international shipping. Ships left Liverpool for west Africa, from where they carried slaves across the Atlantic to the West Indies. On their return voyage to Liverpool they carried sugar and rum. In 1807, just before the British government banned British ships from the slave trade, nearly 200 Liverpool ships took part in it.

THE COTTON TRADE

Liverpool ship-owners soon found a new cargo. The invention of machines for spinning, weaving and printing cotton brought a new industry to Manchester and its surrounding towns. Manchester led the industry so clearly that finished cotton was known as 'Manchester goods'. Raw cotton arrived in bales, or bundles, from the United States – and later from India and Egypt – through Liverpool, and 'Manchester goods' were sent all over the world in the same way. Sugar, rum, tobacco, wheat and timber were other important trades. When the only way of travelling abroad was by sea, Liverpool was also used by ocean liners sailing for all

▼ *British emigrants set sail from Liverpool for North America in 1850. Most emigrants went to North America, but increasing numbers sailed for Australia, New Zealand and Canada.*

THE LEAVING OF LIVERPOOL

From the middle of the 1840s, Liverpool became the port from which hundreds of thousands of people sailed to make a new life for themselves in North America. Many were Irish, fleeing from the poverty of their own country, but large numbers of English, Scots and Welsh families emigrated too. Crammed between the decks of cargo ships, with four people to a space about two metres square, they were at sea for about 40 days. For almost all of them, the pierhead at Liverpool was the last they ever saw of England.

parts of the world.

By 1900, docks and landing-stages lined the northern side of the Mersey estuary close to Liverpool's city centre and stretched for nearly fifteen kilometres. There were docks too at Birkenhead and at Garston. Many food manufacturers, especially those using flour, wheat and sugar such as biscuits and breakfast cereals, built factories close to the ports where these raw materials arrived.

LIVERPOOL'S BUILDINGS

Liverpool became a city of contrasts. There were dreadfully overcrowded slums where families had only one room to live and sleep in, but the owners of businesses connected

◄ *A busy scene at Liverpool Landing-Stage photographed in about 1920. River tugs guided ocean-going liners up the Mersey to the heart of the city, whose streets were lined with warehouses and the offices of shipping companies.*

with the port made huge fortunes. Some of this money was spent on the magnificent buildings for which Liverpool is famous. One is St George's Hall, which housed a concert hall and the Liverpool law courts. Today, it is used as a conference centre and there are plans to restore it. Liverpool's two cathedrals – one Anglican and one Roman Catholic, planned at the beginning of this century but both finished only in the last 30 years – and the Liver Building, built for an insurance company, are other examples.

Meanwhile, the port attracted other industries which set up factories along

the Mersey and the estuary. There were chemical works at Widnes and Runcorn, soap factories at Port Sunlight and Warrington, and later petrochemicals and a car plant at Ellesmere Port. When the Manchester Ship Canal extended seagoing traffic into Manchester, Trafford Park, close to the canal's terminus, became home to over 200 businesses ranging from heavy engineering to flour-milling.

▶ *Today, Liverpool's Landing-Stage serves only the commuter ferries across the Mersey to Birkenhead. The tall building with a clock tower in the background is the Liver Building.*

CHANGING TIMES

Like most of Britain's industrial regions, the Mersey area has faced great changes in the past 30 years.

▲ *Waterfronts in Manchester left derelict by changes in shipping traffic have been redeveloped to provide homes, offices, and leisure and arts facilities. This mixture of homes and offices is at Salford Quays.*

ONE OF THE MAJOR CHANGES has been in sea transport. Today's ships are bigger and their cargoes are more specialised. Cargoes such as grain are shipped in huge bulk carriers. Oil is transported in supertankers. Manufactured goods such as machine parts travel in containers on board specially-designed ships. Modern ships are too large for the old docks and harbours built 100 years or more ago. They need deeper water, more room to dock, and special equipment for loading and unloading quickly.

This was the reason why Liverpool Docks in the city centre closed in 1973 and ships moved to the new Royal Seaforth Dock at

Bootle. This gives direct access to Liverpool Bay in the Irish Sea. Only the Mersey ferries, which carry thousands of passengers daily to work from towns like Birkenhead, use the city-centre terminal. Most of the old docks have been filled in or adapted for new uses. For example, Albert Dock near the city centre now provides the setting for the Liverpool Tate Gallery of modern art, opened in 1988, and the Maritime Museum opened in 1994.

NEARER THE SEA

Similar changes have taken place at the Manchester end of the Ship Canal. Three of the four docks have been cut off from the canal, and are being redeveloped as Salford Quays, a mixture of homes and offices. Work began in the summer of 1997 on an arts centre, due to be opened in 2000, which will contain two theatres, an art gallery and a virtual-reality centre. It will be named the Lowry Centre after L.S. Lowry, the Manchester artist who died in 1976.

▶ *A huge 28-kilometre long sewer laid along the north bank of the Mersey and completed in 1997 plays a vital part in cleaning up the river. It replaces 26 old sewers that discharged household and industrial waste water direct into the Mersey.*

► *A team of volunteers, organised by the Mersey Basin Campaign, clears rubbish from one of the streams that flow into the Mersey. The Campaign runs conservation weekends when volunteers work together to improve the river environment.*

INDUSTRIAL CENTRE

Merseyside is still one of Britain's major industrial areas. Stanlow, south of the estuary, is the second biggest oil refinery in England. Widnes, Runcorn, Port Sunlight, Ellesmere Port and Warrington have large chemical works. There is a major Ford car plant at Halewood, while factories nearby make tyres and other car parts. New industries include a £40 million Sony investment in a Liverpool plant making computer games and interactive video equipment.

BRINGING BACK THE FISH

Meanwhile, Merseyside and Greater Manchester have plans to clean up the rivers, canals and estuary of the Mersey area. The Mersey Basin Campaign is a 25-year project, launched in 1985, which involves schools and volunteer groups as well as businesses. One aim is that by the year 2010 all the rivers and streams in the area will be clean enough to support fish life. So far, fourteen species of fish have returned permanently to the estuary, together with the aquatic plants and organisms on which they feed. The Mersey between Liverpool and Birkenhead is now clean enough to allow an annual cross-Mersey swim – something that would have been dangerous to the swimmers' health only a few years ago.

COMMUNITY FORESTS

Plans for two new 'community forests' covering 1680 square kilometres are part of the Mersey Basin Project. Planting of the Red Rose Forest in Greater Manchester began in 1992. It covers part of the Mersey and several of its tributaries. The Mersey Forest will include the Halton and Warrington areas along the Mersey and land to the south of the estuary at Ellesmere Port. The aim is to plant nearly 20 million trees in the Mersey Forest over the next 25 years.

▼ *The octopus feeds mainly on crabs, which cannot survive in heavily polluted water. Recent sightings of octopus and squid in the Mersey estuary show that the water quality has improved.*

THE LONGEST RIVER

THE SEVERN IS THE LONGEST RIVER IN THE UNITED KINGDOM. IT FLOWS FROM MID-WALES TO THE BRISTOL CHANNEL, WHICH DIVIDES WALES FROM ENGLAND.

THE SOURCE OF THE SEVERN is 610 metres high on the north-eastern slopes of Bryn-Cras, in the Cambrian Mountains. For the first part of its course through the Welsh county of Powys it is also known by its Welsh name, Afon Hafren. Clear and fast-flowing, it falls 457 metres in the first twenty kilometres of its course.

THE SEVERN
Length: 354 km
Source: Bryn-Cras, Cambrian Mountains
Mouth: Bristol Channel
Main tributaries:
Vyrnwy (56 km) meets Severn near Llandrinio
Tern (48 km) meets Severn at Atcham
Worfe (26 km) meets Severn near Bridgnorth
Stour (32 km) meets Severn at Stourport
Teme (96 km) meets Severn at Worcester
Warwickshire Avon (145 km) meets Severn at
    Tewkesbury

▲ *Below Shrewsbury, the Severn takes a wide, meandering course across farmland that is liable to flooding in the winter. Scientists say that this area is the old bed of a lake formed after the last Ice Age as the ice melted.*

ICE AGE CHANGES

Geologists believe that before the last Ice Age, about one million years ago, the Severn flowed north and entered the Irish Sea near where the Mersey reaches the sea today. When ice-sheets crept down from the north, they blocked the old course of the river. The ice reached as far south as the present site of Ironbridge. As the ice retreated, melted water formed a huge lake in this area. Eventually, this overflowed at Ironbridge with such force that it cut a gorge over 100 metres deep. This process exposed coal, limestone, clay and iron ore in the rocks. Thousands of years later, these became the basis of the area's iron-making and pottery industries. From Ironbridge, the Severn found its new route to the Bristol Channel.

The Severn provides the water supply for about six million people who live in the towns and cities along or close to its course. These include Wolverhampton, Dudley, Birmingham and Coventry in the West Midlands and Gloucester and Bristol further south. One of the Severn's Welsh tributaries, the Vyrnwy, which joins it near Llandrinio just inside the Welsh border, supplies piped water to Liverpool.

WINTER FLOODS

On its way south through the counties of Shropshire, Hereford and Worcester and Gloucestershire, the Severn is liable to flooding in the winter months. The water level can rise up to about six metres above normal. Supporters of Worcestershire County Cricket Club claim that the Worcester ground is one of the best in England because it is kept green and fertile by its almost annual flooding.

Below Tewkesbury, the water level is affected by the high tides of the Bristol Channel, which can cause flooding of areas up to 1600 metres wide. The difference between the highest and lowest tides at Avonmouth, on the south side of the Severn estuary, can be as much as fifteen metres. There is only one place in the world, the Bay of Fundy in eastern Canada, where there is a bigger difference. There, it is up to nineteen metres.

South of Gloucester, the Severn begins to widen to form its estuary. After making a wide meander across the flood plain, the estuary stretches for about 70 kilometres until it reaches the Irish Sea.

MEANDERS
1. Slow-flowing river begins to form a loop.
2. The loop widens to become a meander. The outer bank of each curve is undercut.
3. Water breaks through the undercut 'neck' of the meander and finds a new course.
4. A new bank is formed, cutting off the old meander which becomes an ox-bow lake.

river erodes outer banks

river deposits material on inner banks
the meander develops

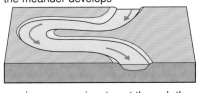
erosion causes river to cut through the narrow neck of land

deposition causes the meander to be blocked off

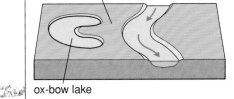
ox-bow lake

▼ *Torrential rain in early January 1998 brought the worst floods on the Severn for over 50 years. This was the scene near Worcester, with the Worcester by-pass carrying traffic across flooded fields.*

THE IRON REVOLUTION

ALTHOUGH THERE IS LITTLE INDUSTRY ON THE SEVERN, A MAJOR EVENT IN THE HISTORY OF IRON-MAKING TOOK PLACE ON THE BANKS OF THE SEVERN IN 1709.

IN THAT YEAR the owner of a small iron works, Abraham Darby, built a new furnace at Coalbrookdale near Shrewsbury. For the first time, the furnace produced iron using coal instead of charcoal as a fuel. First, he partly burnt the coal to get rid of impurities. The result was coke, which was then burnt with iron ore to make iron.

PRODUCING IRON

It was a breakthrough for the iron industry. Most of Britain's forests had been felled to provide charcoal, which had become scarce and expensive. Close to Coalbrookdale, the Severn flowed through the Ironbridge Gorge, where floods following the Ice Age had exposed deposits of coal, limestone and iron ore. There was water power to drive the bellows of the furnace, and the river provided

---

THE FIRST IRON BRIDGE

The world's first iron bridge was built across the Severn near Coalbrookdale by Abraham Darby's grandson. It was opened in 1779, and the small town that grew up round it was called Ironbridge. The bridge, which is 30 metres long, is made entirely of cast iron from the Coalbrookdale foundry. It rises nearly 14 metres above the Severn and was designed to allow river traffic to pass underneath. Now closed to road traffic, the bridge is a historical monument.

▲ *Flat-bottomed trows, special barges designed for use on the Severn, carried passengers and goods between ports along the river. Their masts could be lowered at bridges. When the sails could not be used, trows were dragged along by teams of 'bow-hauliers' from the riverbank.*

▲ *Abraham Darby's bridge over the Severn at Ironbridge. Each part was made in Darby's iron foundry and lifted into place by a hoist on the riverbank. This enabled the bridge to be built without interrupting traffic on the river.*

◀ *Bristol docks in the days of sail. Bristol became a busy port over 800 years ago, but by the nineteenth century, when this photograph was taken, many ocean-going ships were too large to navigate the city-centre docks up the river Avon.*

transport for finished goods. These were needed for Abraham Darby's business, and within 40 years the Coalbrookdale area had become Britain's leading iron producer.

This led to a huge increase in river traffic on the Severn. At that time, the river could be navigated from Welshpool southwards to Bristol, and towns like Gloucester and Worcester were important inland ports. Sailing-barges could carry up to 50 tonnes of cargo, and there were also flat-bottomed barges called 'trows', especially designed for the shifting sands of the river. Trows measured up to eighteen metres and could carry up to eighty tonnes of cargo. But shallow water, sandbanks and rocks made it difficult to sail the lower Severn safely. This led to the building of a canal to allow sea-going ships to sail from Sharpness on the estuary, where new docks

were built, to Gloucester. The canal was opened in 1827 and is still used, though not as much as in the past.

BRISTOL DOCKS

The growth in trade in the nineteenth century led to a huge expansion of the docks at Bristol, which were on the Avon on the south side of the Severn estuary. Bristol's docks were in the centre of the city, and as ships became larger and trade became busier more space was needed. In 1880, new docks were opened at Avonmouth and Portishead on the estuary. Air-raid damage during the Second World War put an end to the useful life of Bristol docks, which have now been converted to a setting for shops, flats, offices, music venues and radio studios.

▶ *Canon's Marsh, the part of Bristol's old docks that has been redeveloped, seen here with a regatta in progress. The large building is a bank office. Close by are an exhibition centre and museums celebrating Bristol's sea-going heritage.*

A CLEAN RIVER

THE SEVERN FLOWS FOR MOST OF ITS LENGTH THROUGH
ROLLING HILLS AND OPEN COUNTRYSIDE. IT HAS SUFFERED LESS
FROM POLLUTION THAN MOST OF BRITAIN'S MAJOR RIVERS.

THE SEVERN HAS VERY GOOD QUALITY WATER, supporting healthy fish and other water life. Below Tewkesbury, where the water level is affected by tides from the Bristol Channel, there is commercial fishing for salmon and eels. The river above Tewkesbury is popular with leisure anglers, who catch salmon and coarse fish such as bream, perch and pike along 1700 kilometres of the riverbanks.

◀ *The Second Severn Crossing, opened in 1996, which carries road traffic across the estuary from Severn Beach near Bristol to Caldicot in Wales. It provides a direct motorway link between London and South Wales.*

FLOOD MEADOWS

The management of the Severn's natural flooding is important to people who live nearby. On the middle Severn, between Stourport and Gloucester, many riverside fields called flood meadows, or 'hams', are allowed to flood each spring, partly to avoid more serious flooding downstream and partly to enrich the soil. Flooding along the estuary, where tidal surges are difficult to forecast, is a greater problem. There will be better protection in 1999, when work is completed on a series of flood walls and banks along a 70-kilometre length of the estuary between Gloucester and Avonmouth.

TIDAL ENERGY

The very high tides that sweep up the Severn estuary from the Bristol Channel represent a natural source of energy that could be harnessed to provide electrical power. The idea of building a Severn Barrage, or dam, which would convert the tidal energy into electricity was first put forward over 70 years ago. The incoming tide would turn the blades of turbines built into the dam. Then the water would be stored behind the dam until the tide began to go out. When the water was released, it would turn the turbine blades again and generate more electricity.

There are only a few places in the world

◀ *At Stonebench in Gloucestershire, young surfers take advantage of the added excitement provided by the Severn Bore. This is a tidal wave that sweeps in from the Bristol Channel, reaching up to two metres high and travelling at an average 16 kilometres per hour.*

where the tides rise and fall enough to generate worthwhile amounts of electricity. The oldest power plant of this kind in the world, opened in 1966, is at Rance in north-western France, where there is a twelve-metre

▼*Wildfowl gathered at the Slimbridge Wildfowl and Wetlands Trust in Gloucestershire. Slimbridge is recognised internationally as an important wetland site, especially for migrating birds which move south from the Arctic Circle for the winter.*

difference between high and low tides. The Severn would be an ideal site for a similar scheme. But although several plans have been put forward in the past 70 years, none has gone ahead. One problem is that of finding a site that would not interfere with shipping. Another is that damming the estuary in this way might have harmful effects on the environment upstream. However, it is still possible that one day electricity will be fed into Britain's homes from the tides of the Severn estuary.

HOME OF THE GEESE

The Severn estuary below Gloucester is an important wetland site recognised by scientists all over the world. It is home to many species of migrating birds, and in particular to the white-fronted goose. This breeds in northern Europe and flies south for the winter. Over 7600 white-fronted geese have been counted in January on the Severn estuary. This is more than half the British population and a quarter of all the white-fronted geese in the world.

TOWARDS TEES BAY

THE TEES RISES AT TEES HEAD ON CROSS FELL IN CUMBRIA. IT FLOWS TO THE SOUTH OF DARLINGTON AND THEN NORTH-EAST TO TEES BAY ON THE NORTH SEA.

THE FIRST PART OF THE COURSE of the Tees is across high, bleak moorland where there are few trees and only scattered and isolated farms and villages. High on the moors is Cow Green Reservoir, completed in 1971. This stores water in the winter and releases it in dry weather to maintain a good flow of water downstream and to provide water for the industrial towns of the lower Tees area.

▲ *High Force, above Middleton-in-Teesdale. The river has cut its way through shale - compressed clay - in two places to reach the plunge pool in the foreground.*

HOW A WATERFALL IS FORMED

The river flows over a ridge of hard rock and the turbulent water and fragments of rock that it carries wear away at the soft rocks below, forming a hollow. This hollow is called a plunge pool.

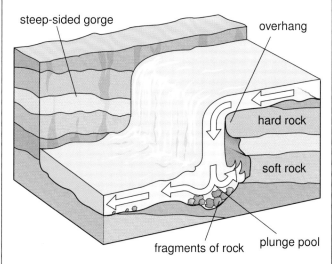

The soft rocks are continually eroded, undercutting the layer of hard rock, which begins to form an overhang. Eventually this overhang collapses. This process is repeated many times, over thousands of years, causing a steep-sided gorge to form.

UPPER TEESDALE

Shortly after it leaves Cow Green Reservoir, the Tees flows over Cauldron Snout, the first of two spectacular waterfalls along its course. The second is about fifteen kilometres downstream at High Force. These waterfalls were formed by water rushing from the moors over ridges of hard rock and cutting away the softer rocks below. Fragments of the softer rocks were carried downstream by the river, and deposited on the river bed and banks.

From High Force, the river widens and flows through a broad valley of farms growing mainly wheat, with few villages or small towns.

THE INDUSTRIAL TEES

As the river meanders round the southern outskirts of Darlington there is a sudden change. The peaceful river of the moors and broad valley becomes an industrial river. It

◀ *Killhope Lead Mine in County Durham, close to tributaries of the Tees, now a museum of lead-mining. Water from abandoned lead-mines in upper Teesdale still sometimes causes local pollution.*

flows on between Stockton-on-Tees and Middlesbrough, where the steel-making and chemical industries are the major activities. Below Stockton-on-Tees, the Tees once flowed slowly across marshland that could not be built on. In the nineteenth century, the river was straightened and the marshland reclaimed for building by draining off the water and giving the land a firm base of heavy industrial waste. But north-east of the industrial areas, towards the North Sea, there are still areas of marsh and mud that are important wildlife habitats, especially for wading birds.

Stockton-on-Tees, Thornaby-on-Tees, Middlesbrough and Hartlepool, on the coast just north of Tees Bay, were all rival ports competing for the chemical and steel industries' trade. With the increasing size of modern ships and the need for specialised handling of different cargoes, these older ports have had to close down and find new uses for their facilities. They have been largely replaced by Teesport on the southern bank of the estuary. The Tees is Britain's third largest port, after London and Milford Haven.

▼ *Teesport, on the south bank of the Tees estuary about three kilometres from the North Sea, was designed to handle large ocean-going ships.*

THE TEES
Length: 112 km
Source: Tees Head, Cumbria
Mouth: Tees Bay, North Sea
Main tributaries:
Lune (20 km) meets Tees near Middleton-in-Teesdale
Skerne (32 km) meets Tees near Darlington
Leven (35 km) meets Tees near Yarm

THE TEES ESTUARY

At the beginning of the nineteenth century, the settlements on the Tees estuary below Darlington were scattered villages and farmhouses on mudflats. By the end, the area was a giant industrial complex.

THE FIRST MOVE for change came in 1825, when the world's first railway was opened between Stockton-on-Tees and Darlington, a journey of about twenty kilometres. Although it carried passengers, its main purpose was to take coal from the Darlington pits to the port at Stockton. From there it was shipped to London. In 1830 the line was extended to Middlesbrough, nearer the sea, where the river was deeper and new docks were being built.

STEEL TOWN

In 1831, just 154 people lived in Middlesbrough. Ten years later the population was nearly 5500, and it went on growing until by 1901 it had reached 91,000.

▲ *The opening of the Stockton to Darlington Railway on 27 September 1825. Crowds gathered all along the 20-kilometre route to see the first train go by. It reached a speed of 24 kph in places.*

Middlesbrough's importance as a port soon faded as new docks for larger ships were built at Hartlepool, just north of Tees Bay and in a sheltered harbour open to the North Sea. But in 1840 Middlesbrough's first iron foundry was opened, and from then on the town's main industry was iron and steel. In 1850, huge deposits of iron ore were discovered at Eston, six kilometres from Middlesbrough. New processes for steel-making followed in the 1870s, and Middlesbrough steel was exported all over the world. One of its most famous products was Sydney Harbour Bridge in Australia, which was opened in 1932 and built entirely of steel parts made in Middlesbrough. Engineering factories using local steel soon spread into the neighbouring Teesside towns.

HEALTH RISKS

The rapid growth of Middlesbrough meant that there was little time for planning. Row after row of tightly-packed, cheap houses were built for the families that flocked to the town for work. There was no drainage system until the 1870s, and no public baths – the workers' houses had no bathrooms – until 1884. The air was badly polluted with chemicals from the ironworks, and on most days a heavy

cloud of black smoke hung over the town. Middlesbrough was an unhealthy place to live, and the death-rate, one of the highest in Britain, proved it.

TEESSIDE CHEMICALS

Chemicals are the other major industry on Teesside. The first chemical works was built at Billingham, north of Middlesbrough, 80 years ago, and it was followed 50 years ago by another at Wilton to the east. In the 1970s, Seal Sands on the north side of the estuary became the site for more chemical works.

The chemical and steel industries are responsible for a large part of the 1,500,000 tonnes of waste produced each year by Teesside industry. Over half of this is dumped at sea after treatment.

MAKING USE OF WASTE

Dumping waste at sea is to be banned from the end of 1998, and another method of disposal must be found. A new waste treatment plant is being built at Bran Sands, south of the Tees estuary, linked by pipelines to sewage works and the major industrial waste producers. When it starts operating in 2002, the plant will collect all the area's waste, treat it and turn it into pellets that can be used as fertiliser or industrial fuel.

▼*Part of the ICI chemical works at Billingham beside the Tees. This was the first chemical plant on Teesside, which started up nearly 80 years ago. The ICI company has another large works at Wilton, east of Middlesbrough, and an oil refinery at North Tees.*

NEW LIFE

THE LOWER TEES IS STILL MAINLY AN INDUSTRIAL AREA, AND TEESSIDE IS STILL A BUSY PORT COMPLEX.

CHEMICALS AND STEEL continue to lead local industry. British Steel employs nearly 7000 workers at its plants near Stockton-on-Tees, Middlesbrough and Hartlepool. The ship-building skills of the people of Teesside have been adapted to build modules for North Sea oil and gas rigs. But new industries have arrived too, such as Cadcam, a company involved in computer-aided design and manufacture.

NEW LIFE FOR OLD DOCKS

The Port of Tees and Hartlepool – mainly the new complex at Teesport on the south side of the estuary – deal with 30 million tonnes of cargo each year. This traffic uses the new quays with their specialised handling equipment, and so new uses have been found for the old docklands and warehouses. At Hartlepool, for example, one old quay has been developed as a shopping mall, Jackson's

Landing, which opened in 1994. Another, Hartlepool Historic Quay, has been turned into a museum. Part of the old harbour has become a marina with berths for up to 750 yachts.

As industries have closed down or moved to new sites, a great deal of land in the Teesside towns has been left derelict. Old industrial land is often polluted by chemicals left behind by processes carried out on the site. This polluted land must be removed and buried at landfills, or dumps, before the sites can be put to new uses. Once this has been done, however, there are opportunities to build exciting new developments close to town centres. Riverside Park in Middlesbrough, which includes a new ground for Middlesbrough Football Club, and the Teesdale shopping centre in Thornaby-on-Tees are examples.

PUTTING THINGS RIGHT

Great damage to the environment has been caused by Teesside's industry in the past. Apart from the pollution of industrial sites, water quality in the Tees estuary suffered badly. By 1970 it was one of the most heavily polluted stretches of water in Britain, lacking in oxygen and almost without life. Air quality, too, was poor because of sulphur dioxide, ammonia and smoke given off mainly by the chemical industry.

◀ *The Marina at Hartlepool, developed from the old harbour.*

THE TEES BARRAGE

The Tees Barrage is a major environmental project at Blue House Point, Stockton-on-Tees. The aim is to improve water quality, prevent flooding and stop the flow of tidal seawater upstream. The first part of the scheme opened in the winter of 1994-95. The Tees has been dammed by the Barrage, although there is a lock to allow boats through and special channels called passes so that migratory fish can move upstream. Upstream of the Barrage is a freshwater lake, which is used for sailing and other watersports.

◀ *Until about 100 years ago, seals were common on the sands of the Tees estuary. Then, because industrial pollution destroyed the fish and shellfish on which they feed, they disappeared. In the 1990s they have begun breeding again on Seal Sands. This common seal, Howie, was found injured on Seal Sands. He was released again into the Tees in January 1997 after four months' care at a local Sea Life Centre.*

The closure of older plants, more care in industry, and tougher laws on pollution have brought great improvements in the past 30 years. Air pollution is now below the safe limits. Pollution is now less than 20% of the 1970 level, which means that common seals are again breeding in the estuary and the hundreds of small organisms that support the food chain for life in the water are returning.

▶ *The Cellnet Riverside Stadium, the headquarters of Middlesbrough Football Club, is built on the site of Middlesbrough docks. The University of Teesside is also expanding along the banks of the Tees to provide room for its 12,500 students.*

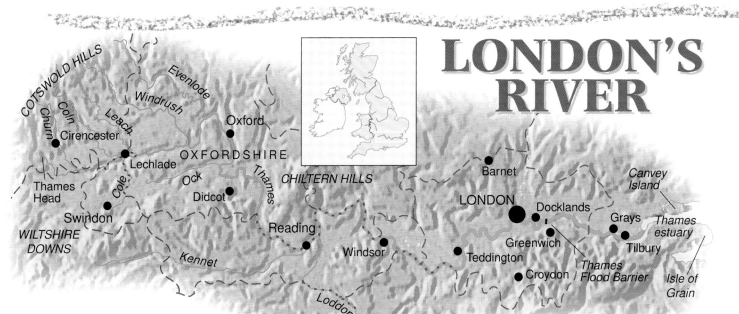

LONDON'S RIVER

THE THAMES IS ENGLAND'S LONGEST RIVER AND THE SECOND LONGEST IN THE UNITED KINGDOM.

THE SOURCE OF THE THAMES is at Thames Head, on the eastern slopes of the Cotswolds about five kilometres from Cirencester. The Thames is a calm, slow-flowing river falling only 108 metres from its source to its estuary, compared with 610 metres on the Severn.

From south of Cirencester it flows east across a broad, shallow valley as far as Oxford. It is joined by many tributaries from the limestone Cotswolds and the chalk Wiltshire Downs. As the Thames moves through its valley it transports its 'load' downstream. The load consists of fine particles of silt suspended in the water and larger particles, such as pebbles and

▲ *The upper Thames flows gently through farming country on the borders of Gloucestershire and Wiltshire.*

▶ *This statue of 'Old Father Thames' used to mark the source of the river at Thames Head. It was created as part of the Great Exhibition held in London in 1851. Today, it is kept at St John's Lock, Lechlade, about six kilometres from the source.*

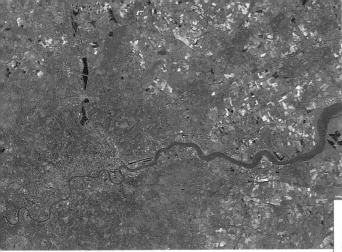

◀ *A satellite image of London from space, using infrared photography that shows vegetation as shades of red, water as dark blue or black and buildings as light blue or grey. The image shows the Thames from Windsor, Berkshire, in the west to Grays, Essex in the east.*

THE THAMES

Length: 338 km
Source: Thames Head near Cirencester, Gloucestershire
Mouth: Thames estuary on the North Sea
Main tributaries:
Leach (30 km) meets Thames near Lechlade, Gloucestershire
Churn (37 km) meets Thames at Cricklade, Wiltshire
Coln (52 km) meets Thames at Inglesham, Wiltshire
Cole (28 km) meets Thames near Lechlade, Gloucestershire
Windrush (48 km) meets Thames near Standlake, Oxfordshire
Kennet (77 km) meets Thames at Reading, Berkshire
Evenlode (68 km) meets Thames near Bladon, Oxfordshire
Ock (37 km) meets Thames at Abingdon, Oxfordshire
Loddon (32km) meets Thames at Wargrave, Berkshire

gravel, that are either rolled or bounced along the river bed. River water also contains a weak acid which attacks rocks, such as limestone and chalk, and dissolves them to form a solution. The river carries this solution to the sea. If the flow of the water is reduced then some of the load, starting with the largest particles such as pebbles, will be deposited on the river bed.

TOWNS ON THE RIVER

The first major town on the Thames is Oxford, the home of one of Britain's oldest universities. The river curves round Oxford, supplying the town's water from the Farmoor Reservoir. South of Oxford is Didcot Power Station, which takes cooling water from the Thames and returns most of it after use. The Thames passes through the wooded Chiltern Hills to another broad valley. It flows through Reading, an industrial town which grew up, like Swindon, when the railway linked it with London in 1835. From Reading onwards, the Thames valley is a corridor for the main road and rail approaches to London from the west.

Thames is surrounded by built-up housing and industrial areas, although some stretches of the banks are free of buildings and used for fishing, watersports and walking.

TIDAL WATERS

From Teddington, in west London, the Thames is tidal, which means that its level rises and falls twice daily with the tides of the North Sea.

▲ *Teddington Lock, 29 kilometres upstream from London Bridge, marks the point below which the level of the Thames is affected by tides from the North Sea. This view looks upstream.*

Passing through the centre of London, the river gradually widens as it reaches its estuary. For the last 30 kilometres of its journey to the sea it passes mudflats, sandbanks and marshes. This estuary land has been built up over thousands of years from deposits of sand and mud carried down the river. Easy access from the North Sea for large tankers has made the estuary a major site for oil terminals and refineries, with Canvey Island on the north shore and the Isle of Grain on the south.

HISTORIC RIVER

THE THAMES HAS BEEN CLOSELY LINKED WITH ENGLISH HISTORY EVER SINCE WILLIAM THE CONQUEROR BUILT HIS FORTRESS, THE TOWER OF LONDON, ON THE NORTH SIDE OF THE RIVER NEARLY 1000 YEARS AGO.

BY 1700, THE THAMES BELOW TEDDINGTON was lined with royal palaces and the great houses of the wealthy. Some, like Hampton Court, Syon House, and parts of the palaces of Westminster and Whitehall, are still there. Many others, along the north bank of the Thames in what is now London's West End, have gone. Upstream from London, Windsor forest became a favourite hunting-ground of William the Conqueror, who built the first royal palace there. In those days, the city of London was a small but busy area close to the river near the present London Bridge. Gradually, it grew until it had taken in outlying villages and it went on growing. Today London is an unbroken network of streets from Barnet in the north to Croydon in the south – a distance of over 30 kilometres, and a similar distance from west to east.

THE GREAT STINK

The Thames still supplies most of London's water, as it has always done. In the past, it was used to carry away human and industrial waste as well. The result was that the river became more and more polluted and unhealthy. Diseases spread when people drank water infected with bacteria. By the 1850s the Thames was the most polluted river in Europe.

In 1858 the London summer was long and hot. The smell of the river became so bad that Members of Parliament, in the House of Commons beside the Thames, had to halt their debates because they could no longer put up with what they called 'the Great Stink'. Soon after

◄ *London's Royal Albert Dock in 1950. The photographer counted 16 cranes and 22 ships! The flat-topped boats in the foreground are Thames 'lighters', which were barges that were used to carry loads upstream as far as Teddington. The Royal Albert Dock is now part of Docklands.*

▶ *A comment by the nineteenth-century cartoonist George Cruikshank on the state of London's water, 'the precious stuff doled out to us'. In fact, the danger to health came not from the organisms shown here, but from microscopic bacteria.*

that, work began on a network of sewers to keep waste water out of the river. Reservoirs were built to the west of London to take supplies from the cleaner water upstream. However, it was not until the 1950s that there were serious attempts to rid the Thames of other sources of pollution, such as industrial waste.

THE PORT OF LONDON

London's sheltered position in the Thames estuary made it a natural site for a port. By the end of the eighteenth century, the river through the City of London was a forest of masts as ships waited to load or unload at the riverside wharves and quays. The need for more space became urgent, and new docks were built on the marshy land downstream from the City. The first docks were opened in 1802, and more were added throughout the nineteenth century. By the 1930s, London was the world's busiest port. It has lost that place now, and is not even in the world's top twenty seaports.

THE BLITZ

During the Second World War, London was heavily bombed – in 1940, for 76 nights running. Nearly 30,000 Londoners died in the raids. Among the buildings badly damaged were the Houses of Parliament, but the bombers' main target was London Docks, which were set ablaze. The docks were surrounded by areas of closely-packed houses, and it was in this area that many of the victims died.

TOWARDS THE MILLENNIUM

OVER THE PAST 50 YEARS, THE LONDON THAMES HAS
BEEN CHANGING RAPIDLY. WAR DAMAGE, THE
RELOCATION OF LONDON'S DOCKS AND NEW
TECHNOLOGY HAVE ALL PLAYED A PART.

THE FIRST BIG NEW DEVELOPMENT came in 1951, when the Royal Festival Hall was opened on the south bank of the Thames on a site that had been laid waste by bombing. Since then, new buildings have been added to the site to make up the South Bank Arts Centre. The centre includes the Hayward Art Gallery, the National Film Theatre and the National Theatre, which has three stages inside one building.

DOCKLANDS

Probably the biggest single change has been in the area of the nineteenth-century docks. The docks became too small and ill-equipped for

modern ships, and London's port trade moved 35 kilometres down the estuary to new docks at Tilbury. One by one, the old docks closed and were abandoned. In the 1970s it was decided to rename the area 'Docklands' and rebuild it as a mixture of homes and offices grouped round the docks. Some of the old warehouses were converted. Others were replaced with new buildings, which include Britain's tallest building, the 244-metre high Canary Wharf Tower. Many large City banks and other firms, as well as several newspapers, have moved their offices to Docklands. The Docklands Light Railway connects the area with the City, and the City Airport provides an air link.

▶ *Canary Wharf Tower dominates the Docklands skyline. The train is running on the Docklands Light Railway, which connects Docklands with the City of London.*

▶ *These aerial views show the Thames Flood Barrier with, in the larger photograph, part of Docklands and the Canary Wharf Tower beyond. The stainless steel structures in the middle of the river contain machinery that raises steel gates whenever there is a danger of flooding.*

THE THAMES FLOOD BARRIER

Over the centuries, the Thames estuary and the lower river have become increasingly liable to flooding. Geologists say that the land mass of Britain is slowly – by about 30 centimetres per century – tilting towards the south-east. As a result, the Thames, which in Roman times 2000 years ago was tidal only as far as London Bridge, is now tidal as far as Teddington.

There have been two bad flood scares in London this century. In January 1928, a tidal surge driven by strong winds swept up the Thames and drowned fourteen people in central London. In January 1953, similar weather brought floodwater within a few centimetres of spilling over.

In 1974, work started on a huge barrier across the Thames near Woolwich, about six kilometres downstream from central London. The Thames Flood Barrier, completed in 1982, consists of a series of steel gates that normally rest on the river bed and allow ships to pass. If there is a flood warning, the gates are raised to form a steel wall that holds back the water. In the first twelve years of operation, the gates were raised twenty times in response to flood alerts.

▼ *An artist's impression of the Dome that will be the centrepiece of the Millennium Exhibition at Greenwich in the year 2000. Over 10 million visitors are expected to visit the Exhibition.*

CELEBRATING THE MILLENNIUM

Britain's main celebrations of the new millennium in the year 2000 will be beside the Thames at Greenwich in south-east London. The Millennium Exhibition will include a domed exhibition building, a terraced walkway along the river, and a new underground station and river-bus jetty for visitors. The site was chosen because the Greenwich Meridian – used all over the world to calculate the time – passes through it.

THE RIVER OF THE MIDLANDS

THE TRENT IS BRITAIN'S THIRD LONGEST RIVER, AFTER THE SEVERN AND THE THAMES. IT IS THE MAIN RIVER OF THE ENGLISH MIDLANDS.

THE TRENT RISES on Biddulph Moor in North Staffordshire and flows for 274 kilometres to meet the Yorkshire Ouse in the Humber estuary on the North Sea. Its course is a long curve, with many changes of direction. Once most of its course was through densely forested country. Today, these forests are only a fraction of their former size. The demand for charcoal from the iron industry before the

▼ *The eighteenth-century bridge across the Trent at Newark. There has been a bridge on this site, next to the castle, since the twelfth century.*

◀ *The Trent and Mersey Canal was designed to link two of England's major rivers and give Midlands' industries outlets for their goods through the port of Liverpool. This is the junction of the Trent and Mersey Canal with the Bridgewater Canal near Runcorn in Cheshire.*

days of coke-fired furnaces, the use of oak in building and shipbuilding, and the spread of towns all caused the forests to shrink.

A TRANSPORT ROUTE

Today, the Trent and its tributaries flow through the heart of manufacturing England, from pottery in Stoke and textiles in Leicester and Nottingham to beer in Burton and cars in Derby. Some of these industries, especially the pottery works, cause severe pollution in the river. Staffordshire, Derbyshire and Nottinghamshire were, from about 1700 to the 1980s, centres of coal-mining, and a few working pits still remain.

The Trent was used as a major transport route by the industries along its banks. The river was backed up by a network of canals, built in the eighteenth century before the age of railways. The longest and best-known of these is the Trent and Mersey Canal, which runs for 150 kilometres from Great Wilne to Preston Brook on Merseyside. It was opened in 1777.

THE TRENT

Length: 274 km
Source: Biddulph Moor, Staffordshire
Mouth: Humber estuary
Main tributaries:
Sow (29 km) meets Trent at Great Haywood, Staffordshire
Tame (48 km) meets Trent near Croxall, Staffordshire
Dove (56 km) meets Trent at Newton Solney, Derbyshire
Derwent (80km) meets Trent at Sawley, Derbyshire
Soar (64 km) meets Trent near Ratcliffe-on-Soar, Nottinghamshire

---

ACROSS FENLAND

From Newark, the Trent flows to Faxfleet, where it joins the Yorkshire Ouse and forms the Humber estuary. The Humber carries the water of the two rivers 60 kilometres, past Kingston-upon-Hull and Grimsby, to the North Sea at Spurn Head.

North Sea tides flowing into the Humber estuary twice a day affect the Trent as far upstream as Cromwell Lock, eight kilometres north of Newark. The rising tides carry sand and mud into the estuary and up the rivers. When the tide falls, some of this sediment is left behind on the river bed. The river also carries sediment downstream towards the estuary. When the river meets the slower moving seawater in the estuary it also deposits its load on the river and sea bed, depositing the heaviest particles first. Over thousands of years, the action of the tides and river has built up a large area of low-lying fenland south of the Humber.

Until banks were built along the rivers and drainage channels were cut across the fens, this was an area of marshland, partly covered with saltwater at high tides and with fresh river water at other times. Today, the drained land makes good pasture for cattle. The remaining saltwater marshland provides a habitat for wildlife such as snails and worms, which live in the mud and come out to feed when the tide comes in. In turn, these creatures are a food source for marshland bird life.

SETTLEMENT AND INDUSTRY

THE VALLEY OF THE TRENT WAS A NATURAL PLACE FOR PEOPLE TO SETTLE. THE RIVER WAS NAVIGABLE, WATER WAS PLENTIFUL AND THE RIVERSIDE LAND WAS FERTILE.

NOTTINGHAM is the largest settlement on the Trent. The Anglo-Saxons, sailing up the Trent from the Humber, founded Nottingham in the sixth century. They lived in caves hollowed out of cliffs overlooking marshland that ran down to the river. In 868 Nottingham was captured by the Danes, and in 924 the first bridge was built there across the Trent.

RAPID GROWTH

Like most industrial towns, Nottingham grew rapidly at the start of the nineteenth century. Between 1780 and 1840 its population trebled to 52,000. The two industries that caused this growth were framework-knitting, a method of knitting cotton cloth, and lace-making. The two were connected, because machines for making lace were developed from the framework-knitting machine by two Nottingham men. Nottingham branched out into other areas of the textile industry, such as bleaching and dyeing, and also into making machines for the industry. Nottingham has always been involved in a number of industrial activities, which has enabled it to avoid the booms and slumps that have troubled one-industry towns, such as pottery-based Stoke-on-Trent.

THE POTTERIES

The pottery industry grew up round Stoke-on-Trent because local coal, needed to fire the kilns, was cheap. Trade grew greatly after about 1730, when pottery began to be made in moulds instead of being 'thrown' on a wheel. The leader of the industry in Stoke was Josiah Wedgwood, who was born in 1730. He helped build the Trent and Mersey Canal which carried raw materials to the potteries and took finished goods away. By 1836 the canal brought to Stoke 70,000 tonnes of clay and 30,000 tonnes of flint a year, and took away 73,500 tonnes of products, which was equal to the weight of about 140 million dinner plates!

◄ Onlookers at the Wedgwood Visitor Centre at Barlaston, Staffordshire, watch an artist applying decoration to pottery before it is sent to the kiln to be fired.

◄ *Nottingham Castle stands on a rock overlooking the town and the Trent. The first castle was built by William the Conqueror 900 years ago, but this was destroyed in 1644 during the Civil War. Today's building dates from the nineteenth century. The statue on the left is of Nottingham's local hero, Robin Hood.*

GENERATING ENERGY

The most obvious sign of industry along the Trent today is the number of power stations and the criss-crossing of the valley by the high voltage transmission lines of the National Grid. The power stations were sited on the Trent because of the availability of local coal as fuel and easy access to the river for cooling water.

▼ *The new gas-fired power station at Keadby on the lower Trent. Gas is cheaper than coal as a fuel for generating electricity. As a result, the few remaining coal-mines in the East Midlands are threatened with closure.*

With the move away from coal as a fuel, some power stations have been demolished, but ten still remain, lining the river from Rugeley to Keadby. The decline in the importance of coal is shown at Keadby, where the old coal-fired power station has been demolished and a new station built in its place, fuelled by North Sea gas.

POLLUTION

In the past power stations caused 'thermal pollution' by releasing warm water that harmed fish and other wildlife. Today power stations have strict controls on the water they release and thermal pollution is rare. Another form of pollution is a greater cause for concern on the Trent. This is caused by the nitrogen used in fertilisers. Nitrogen soaks into the soil and eventually finds its way into rivers and underground water. In the past 60 years, more land has been ploughed and the use of chemical fertilisers has greatly increased. Nottinghamshire is one of ten areas where farmers are experimenting with a reduced usage of nitrogen in the hope of solving the problem.

CHANGES ON THE TRENT

THE TRENT HAS NOT EXPERIENCED THE LARGE-SCALE PROGRAMMES OF RENEWAL AND REBUILDING THAT HAVE AFFECTED THE OTHER BRITISH RIVERS IN THIS BOOK.

THIS IS MAINLY BECAUSE the industrial revolution of the nineteenth century did not do so much damage to the river environment. Also, having no major port, the Trent has not been affected by changes in modern shipping.

Rivers are more than sources of water for homes and industry. They are valuable resources for leisure and sport and people living on the Trent make good use of it.

WATERSPORTS

River-cruising and canoeing have been established pastimes on the Trent for many years. More recent developments have included the setting-aside of zones for water-skiing at six sites along the river.

A focal area for watersports is Holme Pierrepoint, near Nottingham, where a world-class watersports centre has been built. Nearby, at Holme Sluices, there is an international canoe slalom course. Nottingham is a sporting centre in its own right, with two league football club grounds, Notts County and Nottingham Forest, and the Nottinghamshire County Cricket Ground – all recently modernised – overlooking the Trent near Trent Bridge. For walkers, a long-distance path, the Trent Valley Way, runs from Attenborough, south of Nottingham, to West Stockwith near Gainsborough, a distance of about 35 kilometres.

◀ *White-water canoeing at Holme Pierrepoint near Nottingham. The aerial view, left, shows the whole watersports complex, which is used for international events.*

◄ *From Nottingham northwards, the Trent is a favourite river with anglers. They catch many species of fish, but the prize catches are carp weighing up to 14 kilograms.*

THE TRENT AEGIR
The Trent has a tidal bore similar to the Severn Bore, but not as high. It is called the Aegir (pronounced 'eager') after the god of the sea in old northern European myths. The Aegir is a wave that sweeps up the river from the Humber estuary during high tides, sometimes reaching as far inland as Gainsborough. It is strongest after a spell of dry weather when the water level in the Trent is low.

FLOOD PREVENTION

One of the concerns of the Environment Agency, which is responsible for rivers in England and Wales, is flooding on the Trent. There is a long history of flooding going back over 600 years. Newark Bridge was swept away in a flood in 1485, and in 1700 and 1795 floodwater from the Trent spread as far as Lincoln. In this century there were serious floods at various places along the river in 1947, 1953, 1960, 1965 and 1977. Burton-on-Trent, Nottingham and Gainsborough were particularly badly affected in 1947, when 7000 houses in Nottingham and 2000 in Gainsborough were flooded.

Flood-defence schemes carried out since 1947 now protect the stretches of the river most liable to flooding. The largest of these is at Nottingham. New banks and walls have been built along a five-kilometre stretch of the Trent, with a set of floodgates, Holme Sluices, four kilometres downstream from Nottingham. There are five steel gates, each twelve metres wide, and five metres deep. Normally, the gates are lowered into the river, allowing about three and a half metres of water for boats to pass. If there is a flood alert, the sluice gates are raised to let floodwater pass through.

◄ *The sun sets over fields flooded by the Trent at Attenborough, near Nottingham. This is just south of the major flood-prevention scheme designed to protect Nottingham and its suburbs.*

GLOSSARY

ammonia a poisonous gas produced by metal industries such as steel-making

arable farms farms growing crops such as cereals or vegetables

bacteria tiny living creatures, some of which cause disease

barrage a barrier built across a river to reduce the flow of water

bellows a device for blowing air on to a fire to make it burn fiercely

bulk cargo one type of cargo carried loose in the hold of a ship

cast iron iron goods made by pouring molten iron into moulds made of sand

charcoal partially-burnt wood used as a fuel

chromium a metal extracted from certain rocks

coarse fish freshwater fish that are not members of the salmon family

coke partially-burnt coal used as a fuel

container cargo goods transported by land or sea in large metal boxes

drainage basin an area of land of any size or shape that is drained by a river and its tributaries

estuary the wide channel where a river meets the sea

flood plain the flat land of a valley floor over which a river spreads when it floods

furnace a kind of oven in which iron or steel is made

gorge a steep-sided channel cut by a river

Greenwich Meridian an imaginary line round the world which passes through Greenwich and is used to set international time

hydro-electric power energy produced by converting the energy of moving water into electricity

iron ore rock that is heated in a furnace to extract iron

kiln a large oven for hardening pottery

load sediment and rocks moved by a river

marshland (fenland) water-logged low-lying land

meander winding S-shaped bends of a river

migratory fish fish that move from the sea to rivers to breed

mouth (of river) the place where a river meets the sea

mudflat an area of muddy land near an estuary that is covered in water at high tide

pass a sloping channel in a river bed or barrage that allows fish such as salmon to move upstream to breed

petrochemicals chemicals made from oil or natural gas

reaches sections of a river

reservoir a natural or artificial lake used for storing water

sediment ground-down pieces of rock and other material carried along by a river and later deposited on the river banks and bed

source the starting-point of a river

tidal bore a wave produced when high tides are forced up a river estuary

tributary a smaller river that flows into a larger river

wetland site an area of marshland that is a habitat for wildlife

44

INDEX